THE BEST OF
The Beatles

ISBN 978-1-4234-1046-1

Visit Hal Leonard Online at
www.halleonard.com

CONTENTS

ALL MY LOVING

TENOR SAX

Words and Music by JOHN LENNON
and PAUL McCARTNEY

ACROSS THE UNIVERSE

TENOR SAX

Words and Music by JOHN LENNON
and PAUL McCARTNEY

Slowly and smoothly

ALL YOU NEED IS LOVE

TENOR SAX

Words and Music by JOHN LENNON
and PAUL McCARTNEY

AND I LOVE HER

TENOR SAX

Words and Music by JOHN LENNON
and PAUL McCARTNEY

BACK IN THE U.S.S.R.

TENOR SAX

Words and Music by JOHN LENNON
and PAUL McCARTNEY

THE BALLAD OF JOHN AND YOKO

TENOR SAX

Words and Music by JOHN LENNON
and PAUL McCARTNEY

BECAUSE

TENOR SAX

Words and Music by JOHN LENNON
and PAUL McCARTNEY

BIRTHDAY

TENOR SAX

Words and Music by JOHN LENNON
and PAUL McCARTNEY

Moderately fast Rock

BLACKBIRD

TENOR SAX

Words and Music by JOHN LENNON
and PAUL McCARTNEY

CAN'T BUY ME LOVE

TENOR SAX

Words and Music by JOHN LENNON
and PAUL McCARTNEY

COME TOGETHER

TENOR SAX

Words and Music by JOHN LENNON
and PAUL McCARTNEY

Slowly

A DAY IN THE LIFE

TENOR SAX

Words and Music by JOHN LENNON
and PAUL McCARTNEY

DAY TRIPPER

TENOR SAX

Words and Music by JOHN LENNON
and PAUL McCARTNEY

DEAR PRUDENCE

TENOR SAX

Words and Music by JOHN LENNON
and PAUL McCARTNEY

DO YOU WANT TO KNOW A SECRET?

TENOR SAX

Words and Music by JOHN LENNON
and PAUL McCARTNEY

DRIVE MY CAR

TENOR SAX

Words and Music by JOHN LENNON
and PAUL McCARTNEY

Moderately, with a beat

Repeat and Fade

EIGHT DAYS A WEEK

TENOR SAX

Words and Music by JOHN LENNON
and PAUL McCARTNEY

ELEANOR RIGBY

TENOR SAX

Words and Music by JOHN LENNON
and PAUL McCARTNEY

Moderately

EVERY LITTLE THING

TENOR SAX

Words and Music by JOHN LENNON
and PAUL McCARTNEY

THE FOOL ON THE HILL

TENOR SAX

Words and Music by JOHN LENNON
and PAUL McCARTNEY

FROM ME TO YOU

TENOR SAX

Words and Music by JOHN LENNON
and PAUL McCARTNEY

GET BACK

TENOR SAX

Words and Music by JOHN LENNON
and PAUL McCARTNEY

Moderately

GIRL

TENOR SAX

Words and Music by JOHN LENNON
and PAUL McCARTNEY

GOLDEN SLUMBERS

TENOR SAX

Words and Music by JOHN LENNON
and PAUL McCARTNEY

GOOD DAY SUNSHINE

TENOR SAX

Words and Music by JOHN LENNON
and PAUL McCARTNEY

Moderately

GOT TO GET YOU INTO MY LIFE

TENOR SAX

Words and Music by JOHN LENNON
and PAUL McCARTNEY

A HARD DAY'S NIGHT

TENOR SAX

Words and Music by JOHN LENNON
and PAUL McCARTNEY

HELLO, GOODBYE

TENOR SAX

Words and Music by JOHN LENNON
and PAUL McCARTNEY

HELP!

TENOR SAX

Words and Music by JOHN LENNON
and PAUL McCARTNEY

HELTER SKELTER

TENOR SAX

Words and Music by JOHN LENNON
and PAUL McCARTNEY

HERE COMES THE SUN

TENOR SAX

Words and Music by
GEORGE HARRISON

HERE, THERE AND EVERYWHERE

TENOR SAX

Words and Music by JOHN LENNON
and PAUL McCARTNEY

Moderately slow

HEY JUDE

TENOR SAX

Words and Music by JOHN LENNON
and PAUL McCARTNEY

I FEEL FINE

TENOR SAX

Words and Music by JOHN LENNON
and PAUL McCARTNEY

Bright Rock

I AM THE WALRUS

TENOR SAX

Words and Music by JOHN LENNON
and PAUL McCARTNEY

Slowly

I SAW HER STANDING THERE

TENOR SAX

Words and Music by JOHN LENNON
and PAUL McCARTNEY

Moderately bright, with a beat

I SHOULD HAVE KNOWN BETTER

TENOR SAX

Words and Music by JOHN LENNON
and PAUL McCARTNEY

I WANT TO HOLD YOUR HAND

TENOR SAX

Words and Music by JOHN LENNON
and PAUL McCARTNEY

Moderately

I WILL

TENOR SAX

Words and Music by JOHN LENNON
and PAUL McCARTNEY

Moderately

I'LL CRY INSTEAD

TENOR SAX

Words and Music by JOHN LENNON
and PAUL McCARTNEY

I'LL FOLLOW THE SUN

TENOR SAX

Words and Music by JOHN LENNON
and PAUL McCARTNEY

I'M A LOSER

TENOR SAX

Words and Music by JOHN LENNON
and PAUL McCARTNEY

Moderately

I'M HAPPY JUST TO DANCE WITH YOU

TENOR SAX

Words and Music by JOHN LENNON
and PAUL McCARTNEY

I'VE JUST SEEN A FACE

TENOR SAX

Words and Music by JOHN LENNON
and PAUL McCARTNEY

IF I FELL

TENOR SAX

Words and Music by JOHN LENNON
and PAUL McCARTNEY

IN MY LIFE

TENOR SAX

Words and Music by JOHN LENNON
and PAUL McCARTNEY

IT WON'T BE LONG

TENOR SAX

Words and Music by JOHN LENNON
and PAUL McCARTNEY

IT'S ONLY LOVE

TENOR SAX

Words and Music by JOHN LENNON
and PAUL McCARTNEY

Moderately

JULIA

TENOR SAX

Words and Music by JOHN LENNON
and PAUL McCARTNEY

LADY MADONNA

TENOR SAX

Words and Music by JOHN LENNON
and PAUL McCARTNEY

Brightly

LET IT BE

TENOR SAX

Words and Music by JOHN LENNON
and PAUL McCARTNEY

THE LONG AND WINDING ROAD

TENOR SAX

Words and Music by JOHN LENNON
and PAUL McCARTNEY

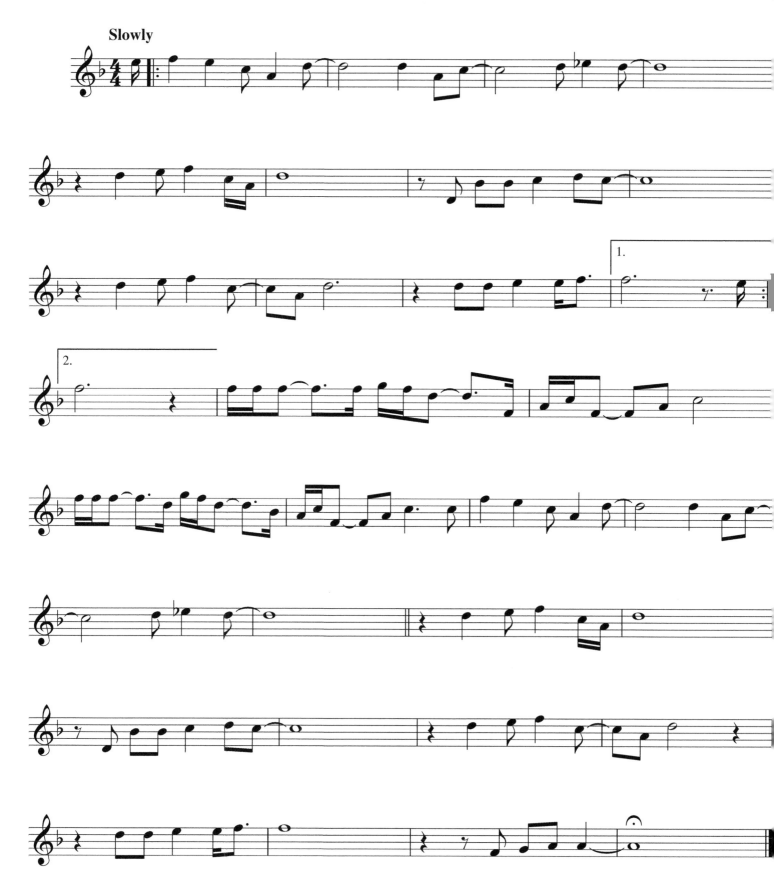

LOVE ME DO

TENOR SAX

Words and Music by JOHN LENNON
and PAUL McCARTNEY

LUCY IN THE SKY WITH DIAMONDS

TENOR SAX

Words and Music by JOHN LENNON
and PAUL McCARTNEY

MAGICAL MYSTERY TOUR

TENOR SAX

Words and Music by JOHN LENNON
and PAUL McCARTNEY

MARTHA MY DEAR

TENOR SAX

Words and Music by JOHN LENNON
and PAUL McCARTNEY

MICHELLE

TENOR SAX

Words and Music by JOHN LENNON
and PAUL McCARTNEY

Moderately

To Coda

1.

2.

D.S. al Coda

CODA

NO REPLY

TENOR SAX

Words and Music by JOHN LENNON
and PAUL McCARTNEY

Moderately

To Coda

1.

2.

1.

2.

D.S. al Coda

CODA

NORWEGIAN WOOD

(This Bird Has Flown)

TENOR SAX

Words and Music by JOHN LENNON
and PAUL McCARTNEY

NOWHERE MAN

TENOR SAX

Words and Music by JOHN LENNON
and PAUL McCARTNEY

OB-LA-DI, OB-LA-DA

TENOR SAX

Words and Music by JOHN LENNON
and PAUL McCARTNEY

OCTOPUS'S GARDEN

TENOR SAX

Words and Music by RICHARD STARKEY
JOHN LENNON and PAUL McCARTNEY

Moderately bright

PAPERBACK WRITER

TENOR SAX

Words and Music by JOHN LENNON
and PAUL McCARTNEY

Bright Rock

PENNY LANE

TENOR SAX

Words and Music by JOHN LENNON
and PAUL McCARTNEY

PLEASE PLEASE ME

TENOR SAX

Words and Music by JOHN LENNON
and PAUL McCARTNEY

P.S. I LOVE YOU

TENOR SAX

Words and Music by JOHN LENNON
and PAUL McCARTNEY

REVOLUTION

TENOR SAX

Words and Music by JOHN LENNON
and PAUL McCARTNEY

RUN FOR YOUR LIFE

TENOR SAX

Words and Music by JOHN LENNON
and PAUL McCARTNEY

SGT. PEPPER'S LONELY HEARTS CLUB BAND

TENOR SAX

Words and Music by JOHN LENNON
and PAUL McCARTNEY

SHE LOVES YOU

TENOR SAX

Words and Music by JOHN LENNON
and PAUL McCARTNEY

SHE'S A WOMAN

TENOR SAX

Words and Music by JOHN LENNON
and PAUL McCARTNEY

SOMETHING

TENOR SAX

Words and Music by
GEORGE HARRISON

STRAWBERRY FIELDS FOREVER

TENOR SAX

Words and Music by JOHN LENNON
and PAUL McCARTNEY

Moderately

TELL ME WHY

TENOR SAX

Words and Music by JOHN LENNON
and PAUL McCARTNEY

Moderately

THANK YOU GIRL

TENOR SAX

Words and Music by JOHN LENNON
and PAUL McCARTNEY

THINGS WE SAID TODAY

TENOR SAX

Words and Music by JOHN LENNON
and PAUL McCARTNEY

THIS BOY
(Ringo's Theme)

TENOR SAX

Words and Music by JOHN LENNON
and PAUL McCARTNEY

TICKET TO RIDE

TENOR SAX

Words and Music by JOHN LENNON
and PAUL McCARTNEY

TWIST AND SHOUT

TENOR SAX

Words and Music by BERT RUSSELL
and PHIL MEDLEY

Moderately, with a beat

WE CAN WORK IT OUT

TENOR SAX

Words and Music by JOHN LENNON
and PAUL McCARTNEY

WHEN I'M SIXTY-FOUR

TENOR SAX

Words and Music by JOHN LENNON
and PAUL McCARTNEY

WHILE MY GUITAR GENTLY WEEPS

TENOR SAX

Words and Music by
GEORGE HARRISON

WITH A LITTLE HELP FROM MY FRIENDS

TENOR SAX

Words and Music by JOHN LENNON
and PAUL McCARTNEY

THE WORD

TENOR SAX

Words and Music by JOHN LENNON
and PAUL McCARTNEY

Moderately

YELLOW SUBMARINE

TENOR SAX

Words and Music by JOHN LENNON
and PAUL McCARTNEY

YES IT IS

TENOR SAX

Words and Music by JOHN LENNON
and PAUL McCARTNEY

Moderately

YESTERDAY

TENOR SAX

Words and Music by JOHN LENNON
and PAUL McCARTNEY

YOU CAN'T DO THAT

TENOR SAX

Words and Music by JOHN LENNON
and PAUL McCARTNEY

YOU WON'T SEE ME

TENOR SAX

Words and Music by JOHN LENNON
and PAUL McCARTNEY

Moderately

YOU'RE GOING TO LOSE THAT GIRL

TENOR SAX

Words and Music by JOHN LENNON
and PAUL McCARTNEY

YOU'VE GOT TO HIDE YOUR LOVE AWAY

TENOR SAX

Words and Music by JOHN LENNON
and PAUL McCARTNEY

Moderately

YOUR MOTHER SHOULD KNOW

TENOR SAX

Words and Music by JOHN LENNON
and PAUL McCARTNEY